A Note to Parents and Teachers

Eyewitness Readers is a compelling new reading programme for children. *Eyewitness* has become the most trusted name in illustrated books and this new series combines the highly visual *Eyewitness* approach with engaging, easy-to-read stories. Each *Eyewitness Reader* is guaranteed to capture a child's interest while developing his or her reading skills, general knowledge and love of reading.

The books are written by leading children's authors and are designed in conjunction with literacy experts, including Cliff Moon M.Ed., Honorary Fellow of the University of Reading. Cliff Moon spent many years as a teacher and teacher educator specializing in reading. He has written more than 140 books for children and teachers and he reviews regularly for teachers' journals.

The four levels of *Eyewitness Readers* are aimed at different reading abilities, enabling you to choose the books that are exactly right for each child.

Level One   Beginning to read
Level Two   Beginning to read alone
Level Three   Reading alone
Level Four   Proficient readers

The "normal" age at which a child begins to read can be anywhere from three to eight years old, so these levels are intended only as a general guideline.

No matter which level you select, you can be sure that you're helping children learn to read, then read to learn!

A Dorling Kindersley Book

Project Editors Mary Atkinson
and Carey Combe
Art Editor Karen Lieberman
Senior Editor Linda Esposito
Production Josie Alabaster
Photography Ray Moller

Reading Consultant
Cliff Moon M.Ed.

Published in Great Britain by
Dorling Kindersley Limited
9 Henrietta Street
London WC2E 8PS

2 4 6 8 10 9 7 5 3

Visit us on the World Wide Web at http://www.dk.com

Eyewitness Readers™ is a trademark of
Dorling Kindersley Limited, London.

A CIP catalogue record for this book is
available from the British Library.
ISBN 0-7513-5856-8

Colour reproduction by Colourscan, Singapore
Printed and bound in Belgium by Proost

The publisher would like to thank the following:
Animal Ark for supplying the puppy;
Demi Gray, Jack Gray, Francesca Agati,
and Christopher Gunning for modeling.

The publisher would also like to thank the following for
their kind permission to reproduce the photographs:
Eye Ubiquitous: 27 t; Robert Harding: 27 b.

EYEWITNESS ◉ READERS

Level
1
BEGINNING TO READ

Surprise Puppy!

Written by Judith Walker-Hodge

DK

DORLING KINDERSLEY

London • New York • Moscow • Sydney

On Friday afternoon,
Dad brought home
a surprise.

"Look what I've got," he said.
"It's a puppy!
He belongs
to a friend
of mine."

"Will you help look after him for a week?"

"Yes! Yes!"
shouted the twins.

puppy

"The puppy's wagging his tail," said Sam.

"That means he likes us," said Jessica.

"My friend wants you to give him a name," Dad told the twins.

"I want to call him Wags," said Jessica.

"Wags is a good name," said Sam. "He wags his tail a lot."

Wags ran around the room.

"He wants to play," said Dad.
"He needs lots of exercise."

Sam looked in the box of things
that had come with Wags.
He found a toy ball.

He threw the ball
into the garden.
"Fetch," he called.

Wags chased the ball, but ...

... he did not bring it back.

He just sat
by the ball and
wagged his tail!

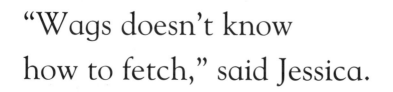

"Wags doesn't know
how to fetch," said Jessica.

"Let's teach him this weekend,"
said Sam.

"Good idea," said Dad.
"Then next week
you can show my friend
what he can do."

Later that evening,
Dad couldn't find
his slippers.

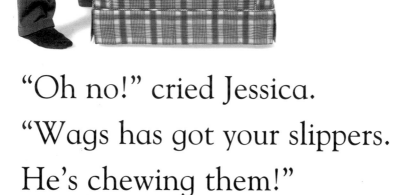

"Oh no!" cried Jessica.
"Wags has got your slippers.
He's chewing them!"

"He's teething,"
Dad told her.

"Give him a dog chew.
There's one in the box
with his things."

chew

Soon it was bedtime.
"Can Wags sleep with me?"
Sam asked.

"Wags is too young," said Dad.
"He has to sleep in the kitchen."

"Put some newspaper
on the floor in case
he makes a mess."

"Make sure
he has water,"
said dad.

"Then lay a blanket
in his basket
to keep him warm."

basket

On Saturday morning,
the twins rushed
into the kitchen.

Wags jumped up at them.
He was pleased
to see them.

"Get down, Wags,"
said Mum.
"Puppies must learn
not to jump up
at people."

"Do puppies eat cornflakes?"
asked Sam.

"Don't be silly.
Puppies eat puppy food,"
said Jessica.
"Mum is feeding Wags now."

Mum filled Wags's
food bowl
with puppy food.

Then she filled
his water bowl
with fresh water.

bowl

That afternoon,
they went to the vet.
Wags needed a check-up.

"Why do you need
to check Wags?" asked Sam.

"To make sure
he is healthy,"
said the vet.

vet

The vet checked Wags carefully.

"Wags has a shiny coat
and a wet nose.
That means
he's well,"
she said.

On Sunday,
the family took Wags
for a long walk.
They went to the park.

Sam and Jessica took turns holding the lead.

"I wish we had a puppy," said Jessica.

"Puppies are hard work," Dad told her.

"We don't mind!" shouted the twins.

lead

After the walk,
everyone went indoors.

Jessica hung Wags's lead
on the coat rack.

Sam put some
fresh water in
the water bowl.

No one noticed that
the gate was open.

No one ...
except Wags!

"Where's Wags?"
Dad asked
a few minutes later.

"Oh no,
the gate's open!"
cried Jessica.
"Wags has
run away."

"Come on,
let's find him,"
said Mum.

But he wasn't on the street.

And he wasn't in the park.

"I've found him!" called Jessica.
Wags was next door.
He had been rolling
in the mud.

They brought him home and
gave him a bath.

"We have to keep
the gate shut,"
Mum told
the twins.

"Okay," said Jessica
as she dried Wags with a towel.

"Sorry," said Sam.
Then he brushed Wags
with a dog brush.

towel

On Monday,
it was the
twins' birthday.

Mum gave them a tiny box
and Jessica opened it.

"It's a tag!" she said.
"It has our address on it ...
and it says WAGS!"

"It's a dog tag,"
said Dad.
"Wags belongs
to you two now.
This weekend was a test.
You passed with flying colours!"

dog tag

Picture Word List

puppy

page 5

vet

page 21

chew

page 13

lead

page 23

basket

page 15

towel

page 29

bowl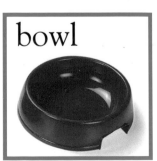

page 19

dog tag

WAGS

page 31